ROMAN CHESTER

by

T. J. Strickland

First edition July 1984
Second impression November 1986

Published by Hendon Publishing Company Limited, Hendon Mill, Nelson, Lancashire.
Printed by Fretwell & Cox Ltd., Goulbourne St., Keighley, West Yorkshire, BD21 1PZ.

CONTENTS

ACKNOWLEDGEMENTS

Drawings of the Antefix tile, helmet cheek-piece, dagger blade and scabbard, mess-tin handle, lead tag, amphora label and horse-headed buckle ornament by Peter Alebon.

Photographs by Thomas Ward.

The French and German translations of the summary were done by Sybil Graham.

Front cover: The defences of *Deva* as they might have appeared in *c.* AD 200. (G. Sumner).
Back cover: Much of the Roman masonry survives today in the north wall of the City of Chester.

PLACES MENTIONED IN THE TEXT

Modern name	Roman name
Western coast of Greece	*Actium*
Bangor-on-Dee	*?*
Caerleon	*Isca (castra legionis)*
Chester	*Deva (castra legionis)*
Colchester	*Camulodunum*
Cologne	*Colonia Ara Agrippinensis*
Grampian Mountains	*Mons Graupius*
Holt	*Bovium?*
Inchtuthil	*Victoria*
Lincoln	*Lindum*
Mainz	*Moguntiacum*
Mancetter	*Manduessedum*
Neuss	*Novaesium*
Ravenna	*Ravenna*
Rome	*Roma*
Whitchurch (Shropshire)	*Mediolanum*
Wroxeter	*Viroconium*
R. Dee	*Deva*
Solway Firth	*Ituna*
R. Tyne	*Tinea*
R. Ribble	*Belisama?*
R. Tay	*Tava*

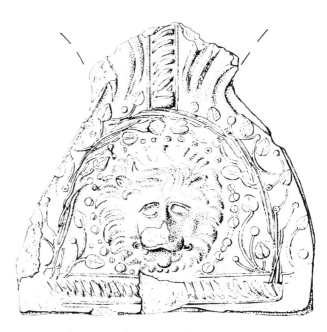

A fine example of an Antefix tile from *Deva*.

EMPERORS AND OTHERS MENTIONED IN THE TEXT

A Roman soldier's brooch.

Emperors	Dates
Claudius	AD 41-54
Nero	54-68
Vespasian	69-79
Titus	79-81
Domitian	81-96
Trajan	98-117
Hadrian	117-138
Antoninus Pius	138-161
Severus	193-211
Caracalla	211-217
Trajan Decius	249-251
Carausius	287-295
Allectus	295-296
Constantine	308-337
Magnentius	350-353

Others	
Julius Caesar	100 BC-44 BC
Queen Boudicca	AD 60
Gnaeus Julius Agricola	40-93
Constantius Chlorus	250-306
Magnus Maximus	-388
Arthur	c. 450-c. 500
Saint Augustine	-605
Aethelfrith of Northumbria	-617

Tribesmen	Approximate Territory
Brigantes	Northern England
Iceni	Norfolk area
Ordovices	Central and northern Wales
Deceangli	North east Wales

THE CHESTER REGION IN ROMAN TIMES

Key:

■   Legionary Fortress: *Deva*

■   Auxiliary Forts: 1. Manchester
                              2. Northwich
                              3. Whitchurch

□   Possible military site: 4. Wilderspool

●   Settlements: 5. Meols
                          6. Saltney
                          7. Heronbridge
                          8. Middlewich

○   Holt Factory

V   Villa near Tarporley

◊   Bangor-on-Dee (Dark Age monastery)

△   Other Sites:
      9. Pentre 10. Near Tilston
      11. Kelsall 12. Near Tushingham
      BRIGANTES   Tribe
      ——— -----   Roads, certain and possible

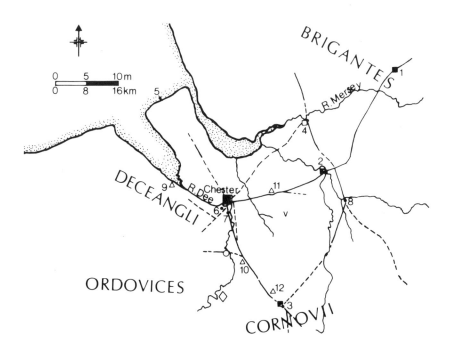

MAP OF BRITAIN

Key:

1   Grampian Mountains
2   Inchtuthil
3   Antonine Wall
4   Hadrian's Wall
5   York
6   River Ribble
7   Lincoln
8   Chester
9   Wroxeter
10   Battle, Mancetter area, AD60
11   Colchester
12   Caerleon
      ■ = Legionary Fortress

PLAN OF LEGIONARY FORTRESS OF *Deva*

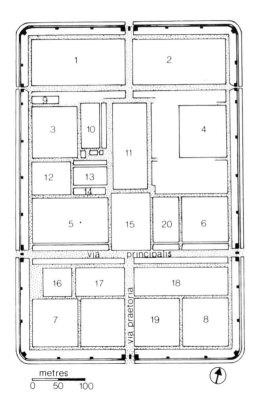

Key:

1–8	Barracks
9	Granary
10	Stores Depot?
11	Hospital?
12	Workshops
13	Elliptical Building
14	Bath house
15	Headquarters
16	Granaries
18	Tribunes' Houses
19	Bath-building and exercise hall
20	Legionary commander's palace?

From the outset until the early third century a series of cook-houses and mess-huts were located just inside the defences.

CHESTER: CITY CENTRE MAP

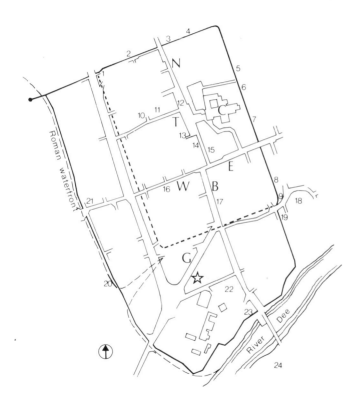

Key:

Some principal streets and buildings in the modern city

N	Northgate Street
T	Town Hall
C	Cathedral
E	Eastgate Street
B	Bridge Street
W	Watergate Street
G	Grosvenor Street
☆	Grosvenor Museum
	(major displays of Roman Chester)

The City Wall is shown as a thick black line.
The west and south sides of the Fortress are shown with a broken line.

Features of Roman Chester still to be seen

1   North west Angle tower (marked in pavement)
2,3,4   Impressive lengths of the Fortress wall incorporated in the City Wall
5,6   Fortress wall (both sides of Kaleyard Gate)
7   Fortress wall (Mercia Square)
8   Fortress wall (behind 12, St John Street)
9   South east Angle tower (foundations on display)

Fortress Buildings

10   Barracks (marked in pavements)
11   Possible Stores Depot (marked in pavements)
12   Possible Hospital (marked in pavements)
13   Strongroom in Headquarters Building (Hamilton Place)
14   Headquarters Building columns (in cellar of 23, Northgate St)
15   Hypocaust of unidentified building (12, Northgate Street)
16   Column for a possible Tribune's House (35, Watergate Street)
17   Bath building hypocaust (39, Bridge Street)

Outside the Fortress

18   Amphitheatre
19   Roman Garden (stones collected from various Roman buildings)
20   Quayside Wall (marks the line of the Roman waterfront)
21   Furnace arches for hypocaust (basement of 104, Watergate Street)
22   Well of official post-house, *Mansio,* (garden of 5, Castle Place)
23   Roman mains culverts (under carpark, 3-5, Shipgate Street)
24   Shrine of Minerva and Roman quarries (Edgar's Field, Handbridge)

2, 8, 14, 21, 22, 23 can only be seen by prior arrangement with the owner/proprietor concerned. Small groups recommended.

INTRODUCTION

This history of Roman Chester is not intended to be an exhaustive study of the subject. Rather it is designed to give a general, but nevertheless accurate historical outline. It is more than ten years since the last account was written and during that period — for the first time in Chester — a team of professional full-time archaeologists has been continuously active in Chester. Thus there have been great advances in knowledge of the period and it is important that the general reader and visitor to Chester knows what these are.

Before reading on, it is worth pausing to consider one or two points which are not generally appreciated. Firstly, we should remember that a time as long as that which separates us from Tudor England, divided the inhabitants of fifth-century Chester from those of the first century. Changes at least as great as those which have taken place in the last four hundred years took place during the Roman period, but we would be wrong to imagine that the inhabitants of late Roman Chester were any the less 'Roman' for all that. Over the centuries the population of Roman Chester, civilians and soldiers alike, became increasingly mixed in racial composition, largely due to marriages with the native British of the area. From the

third century onwards there would, too, have been a steady increase in what may loosely be described as the Germanic elements. Undoubtedly, there were exceptions, but in general the racial composition of the great majority of the people of Chester by the fourth century would have been rather similar to that of the present day population — a thorough mixture of Celtic and Germanic and some 'mediterranean' strains. It would be incorrect, therefore, to use the term 'Roman' in a racial sense; it is better used to refer to the period during which Chester came under the jurisdiction and control of Roman government.

Secondly, let us remember that great historic cities like Chester contain something of the total history of Britain, and thus hold within their fabric an incomparable wealth of fascinating and important information concerning all historical periods. Archaeological teams, like the one in Chester, have a highly developed sense of responsibility for the cities in their care. They feel, too, that their particular city is not unlike a unique and priceless book, the pages of which are constantly being torn out by modern urban redevelopment, and which they have to learn to read and record for posterity, sometimes under particularly distressing conditions. At the same time — and contrary to the opinions held by some people — their profession gives them a strong belief in what they call the continuity of society and hence in the inevitability of progress and change. Most archaeologists do not want to turn their 'charges' into open-air museums — but they do want to preserve a balance between conservation and total destruction. Most people will agree that one of the worst characteristics of the times in which we now live is the far-too-rapid rate of change which leads to a sense of insecurity. Archaeology helps us to preserve a balance as well as to learn about ourselves and where we are going.

Tim Strickland, December 1983

Hinged buckle from Legionary armour.

CHAPTER ONE: THE EARLY YEARS

JULIUS CAESAR

Most people know that Julius Caesar came to Britain in 55 and 54 BC. What is less readily appreciated is that, although Caesar achieved little more than a reconnaissance in the south-eastern part of the country, the people of Britain then came under the influence of Rome more completely than would otherwise have been possible. For the next hundred years the hand of Rome was felt increasingly in all but the remotest parts of the island — but this was not the hand of conquest so much as that of political and commercial influence. Although as yet we lack the proof of this at Chester, we may be sure that the salient features of the geography of the region, and the potentialities of this site in particular, were well known to at least the more adventurous among the trading fraternity.

THE INVASION OF CLAUDIUS AND ITS AFTERMATH

In AD 43, nearly a hundred years after Caesar's brief expeditions to Britain, the Emperor Claudius confronted a deteriorating political situation in southern Britain which made necessary the invasion and conquest of the south-eastern parts of the country. Within ten years or so of the invasion, units of the Roman Army were active in the Chester area, and at this time, probably on more than one occasion, the great possibilities of the site at Chester were put to good, if temporary, use. In AD 60 the Roman Army was active in north Wales when southern Britain was plunged into upheaval by the rebellion of Boudicca (Boadicaea), and complete conquest of the region was brought to an abrupt halt and deferred for some years to come.

This cremation urn may have been placed in a cemetery outside a regimental fort prior to the construction of the legionary fortress.

The Emperor Nero, AD 54-68.

THE ARRIVAL OF *LEGIO II ADIUTRIX*

A few years later, after the death of the Emperor Nero, the Roman World was drawn again into civil war which came to an end in AD 70 with the rise of Vespasian to imperial power. It was under his direction that a new forward policy of total conquest of Britain was formulated. As part of the preparations for the conquest of northern Britain — and perhaps of Ireland also — the site of Chester came at last to be permanently occupied by the Roman Army, and *Legio II Adiutrix* (the Second 'Auxiliary' Legion) was sent from Lincoln to construct a new legionary fortress at Chester.

HISTORY OF *LEGIO II ADIUTRIX PIA FIDELIS*

This was originally an 'auxiliary' legion raised by Vespasian from the men of the imperial fleet based at Ravenna during the Civil War of AD 69. He honoured it for its loyalty with the title '*Pia Fidelis*' (Loyal and Faithful) and made it a permanent legion. In AD 70 it was posted to the German Frontier; then in the following year it was sent to Britain and took over the old fortress of the Ninth Legion at Lincoln. A short time later it was transferred to Chester, where the earliest surviving inscriptions confirm that parts of this fortress were under construction in AD 79, during the governorship of Gnaeus Julius Agricola.

THE MEN OF *LEGIO II ADIUTRIX*

Several tombstones of men of the Second Legion have survived to this day. Inscriptions on these stones give brief details of the military careers, ancestry and ages of these men, many of whom came from those parts of the Roman world which are now parts of northern Yugoslavia and northern Italy.

The Emperor Vespasian, AD 69-79.

Legionary tombstone. Translated, it reads:

GAIUS CALVENTIUS CELER, SON OF GAIUS, OF THE CLAUDIAN VOTING TRIBE, FROM APRUS. SOLDIER OF THE SECOND LEGION ADIUTRIX PIA FIDELIS, IN THE CENTURY OF VIBIUS CLEMENS . . . (Aprus was a colony in Thrace).

WHY THE FORTRESS WAS BUILT AT CHESTER

Nowadays, the landscape is so greatly changed and built up that it is not easy to appreciate what the advantages of the site were; but to the Romany Army they would have been very obvious. Probably the most important reason for locating the fortress at Chester was the River Dee which, at that time, was navigable right up to the sandstone ridge on which the new base was being constructed. This provided superb harbour facilities for the large-scale supply by sea of the Army in its northward progress. This was also the lowest crossing point of the river, with reasonable overland communication to the south and east. A bonus was the position of the site between the recently subjugated, and still restive, tribesmen of the ORDOVICES in Wales, and the still hostile territories of the BRIGANTES to the east and north. Although this is not often said, it seems possible that Chester was to have been used as a supply base and embarkation point in the intended conquest of Ireland, which in this period was considered to be within the grasp of the Roman Army.

Iron scale armour.

THE FIRST FORTRESS

Legio II Adiutrix constructed a fortress of just under sixty acres (24 hectares) in size, surrounded by defences which included a rampart, wooden towers and gates, and a ditch outside. The new fortress was appreciably larger than the other permanent legionary fortresses in Britain, a fact which has not yet been adequately explained. Within the defences the majority of the buildings were of wooden construction, frequently of wattle-and-daub, but it would be a mistake to imagine that

Iron cheek piece from a late first-century legionary helmet.

Opposite: The legionary bath house, as it might have appeared in AD 79.

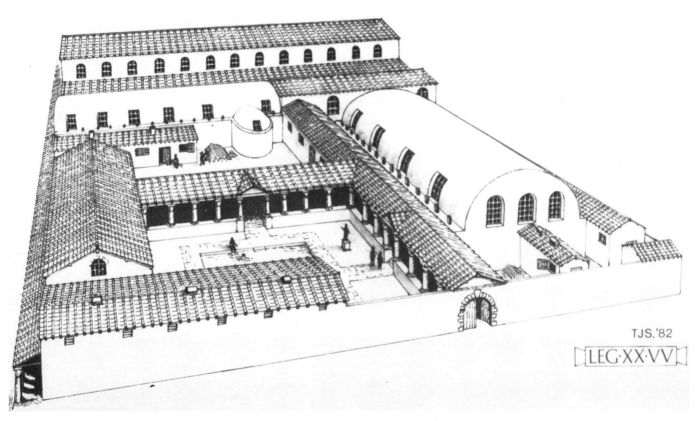

TJS.'82

LEG·XX·VV

15

they were in any way makeshift. Recent discoveries of decorated wall plaster in some barracks of this period show them to have been finished to a high standard.

Certain of the fortress buildings were constructed of locally quarried sandstone almost from the beginning of permanent occupation. Amongst these were the baths and, possibly, the enigmatic 'Elliptical Building'. However, the latter appears not to have been completed at that time. Wells were sunk, and springs to the east of the site were tapped as the main sources of running water; and lead water pipes were provided for internal distribution to the more important buildings.

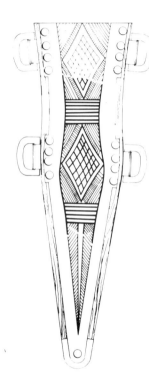

First-century dagger scabbard. Iron, inlaid with silver or tin.

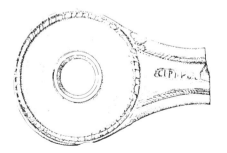

Bronze mess-tin handle. Made by CIPIVS POLYBIVS in southern Italy.

WHAT THE ROMANS CALLED CHESTER

They called the fortress *Deva,* a word which was derived from the Celtic name of the River Dee. However, we can be sure that the soldiers, in their attempts at copying what they thought they had heard, mispronounced the name by which Chester was formally known thereafter! Very quickly it was referred to as '*Castra Legionis*' — the legionary fortress — and this name lasted into the early Middle Ages as '*Legaceaster*'. It is from this that the present name 'Chester' is derived.

THE DEPARTURE OF *LEGIO II ADIUTRIX*

In AD 83 the Emperor Domitian (the younger son of Vespasian) withdrew part of the legion to the Rhine frontier. Soon after this there was serious trouble in the Danube region and further military reinforcements were required there.

Legio II Adiutrix was in 'reserve' at Chester and was considered to be the legion most easily spared from the garrison of Britain. In about AD 87 its remaining fighting strength departed for the Continent. With wisdom of hindsight we know that this legion never returned, but it is likely that this was not expected at the time, and the fortress at Chester probably remained under the nominal control of the Second Legion for a few years to come. However, apart from administrative and training staff, and recruits, there would not have been many troops who remained behind.

Above, left: Coin of the Emperor Domitian, AD 81-96.

Right: A legionary dagger blade.

A room in the house of a senior centurion of the First Cohort of the legion in the late first century AD. A reconstruction based on wall plaster recovered in 1973. (G. Sumner).

17

THE WITHDRAWAL FROM SCOTLAND IN THE LATE FIRST CENTURY

Although *Legio II Adiutrix* had been in reserve, its withdrawal from Britain was a major factor behind the decision to halt the process of total conquest of the north. During the reigns of Vespasian and his son Titus, the provincial governor, Gnaeus Julius Agricola, had achieved some notable successes as far north as the edge of the Grampian mountains. By AD 87 the army was well into the process of establishing itself in that region of Scotland in permanent positions, of which perhaps the most famous was the new legionary fortress at Inchtuthil on the River Tay. However, the withdrawal of the Second Legion from Chester removed the vital reserve element from the northern army which, henceforth, was too thinly spread to hold the conquered territories, let alone the passes radiating from the unconquered Highland Massif. In the space of a few years, therefore, the Army was forced to give up its northern conquests and gradually withdrew to a line which could be held by a smaller provincial garrison. The legions which had been directly involved in the north withdrew to fortresses well to the rear, and one of them, *Legio XX Valeria Victrix* (the Brave and Victorious Twentieth), withdrew temporarily to its fortress at Wroxeter *(Viroconium)*.

HISTORY OF *LEGIO XX VALERIA VICTRIX*

This legion had been raised by Augustus after the Battle of Actium in 31 BC. Early in the first century AD it was stationed at Cologne and then Neuss, on the Rhine. It took part in the invasion of Britain in AD 43, after which it was stationed at Colchester for a few years. Together with the Fourteenth Legion, part of the Twentieth defeated Boudicca (Boadicaea), Queen of the

The fortress defences *c.* AD 100.

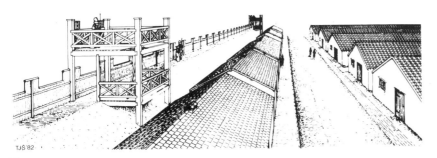

TJS 82

ICENI, in the Midlands, possibly near Mancetter, in AD 60. For its part in this decisive victory it was honoured with the title *'Valeria Victrix'* (Brave and Victorious). From the later 60s the Twentieth Legion was based at Wroxeter.

THE ARRIVAL OF *LEGIO XX VALERIA VICTRIX*

During the early 90s it was decided that *Legio II Adiutrix*, still nominally in control of Chester, would not be returning there. Thus the fortress became available to the Twentieth Legion, which moved northwards to occupy it, at the same time dismantling its former base at Wroxeter. On arrival in Chester, the Twentieth Legion took over the fortress, which had been built some fifteen years previously. Clearly, much of it, including the defences, needed repair, rebuilding or alteration. In some cases, such as the legionary amphitheatre outside the fortress, earlier timber buildings were rebuilt in stone. Essentially, however, the fortress retained the same layout and characteristics as before. A new feature at this time was a series of mess-huts and cook-houses around the periphery of the fortress and just inside the rampart. To aid them in their rebuilding programme, and to satisfy their demands for pottery on a large scale, the legionaries established a large tile and pottery factory at Holt *(Bovium)*, a few miles up the River Dee. As with the earlier occupants, a number of remarkable inscribed tombstones have survived at Chester. These inscriptions show that men of the Twentieth Legion came from colonies in Spain, southern France, Yugoslavia and northern Italy.

Rampart turves. The rampart consisted of a rubble core and turf revettments, bonded together with timber.

Roof tiles made by the Twentieth Legion at Holt.

[LEG·XX·VV]

TJS '82

THE FORTRESS IN THE EARLY SECOND CENTURY

In the first twenty years or so of the second century the legion continued the gradual process of conversion of buildings from timber to stone. Amongst the structures to be so treated were the defences, a fact possibly recorded on a fragment of an official inscription which may once have come from one of the new gates of the fortress. The wooden gates, towers and palisade were completely replaced in stone, and a new stone curtain was added to the front.

Barracks of the Twentieth Legion. Early second century.

Foundations of a stone tower set in the pre-existing rampart *c.* AD 110-120.

The defensive ditches were recut. Undoubtedly, systematic rebuilding of the entire fortress was intended, but in about AD 125 the programme seems to have been brought to an abrupt halt and many buildings were left incomplete, whilst conversion of others had not even started. This is not to say that the fortress ceased to be occupied, because continued rubbish disposal attests continued use, but clearly something drastic had happened. This was the time of the Emperor Hadrian's visit to Britain, and it was he who decided to set a permanent limit to the territory of the Roman province and, as his biographer tells us, to 'separate Roman from Barbarian'. Thus, the great frontier works which have come to be known as Hadrian's Wall were constructed across northern Britain between the Solway Firth and the Tyne estuary.

Inscriptions tell us that, amongst others, the men of the Twentieth Legion had much to do with the construction of this great wall. We may safely assume that large numbers of men — if not the entire 'field' force of the legion — were engaged upon construction of the new frontier works, and this is the explanation of the apparent cessation in building activity at Chester.

A legionary stores building c. AD 120. (G. Sumner)

The Emperor Hadrian, AD 117-138.

HADRIAN'S WALL AND THE ANTONINE WALL

During the reign of Hadrian's successor, the Emperor Antoninus Pius, the policy for northern Britain was changed to include, once again, the holding of Britain as far north as the Forth-Clyde isthmus, and a new system of frontier works, known today as the Antonine Wall, was constructed. At the same time Hadrian's Wall was largely abandoned. The new frontier was, as before, the work of the legions including the Twentieth. There is, too, some evidence to show that the legions provided men for more-or-less permanent garrisons for some of the northern forts in this period and several decades to come. During this long interval Chester was used as a rearward depot in which, amongst other things, military equipment appears to have been both manufactured and repaired for supply to the northern garrisons. It was not until *c.* AD 165, with the withdrawal from Scotland and the recommissioning of Hadrian's Wall, that the Twentieth Legion may be supposed to have been detailed to return in strength, though not in its entirety, to Chester.

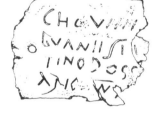

Inscribed luggage tag, made of lead. Translated it reads:

NINTH COHORT. PROPERTY OF LUCIUS VANIUS, FOR SETINUS, BY BAGGAGE ANIMAL.

Legionary tombstone. Translated, it reads:

TO THE SPIRITS OF THE DEPARTED AND TO PUBLIUS RUSTIUS CRESCENS, OF THE FABIAN VOTING TRIBE, FROM BRIXIA. SOLDIER OF THE TWENTIETH LEGION VALERIA VICTRIX, AGED 30, OF 10 YEARS SERVICE. GROMA, HIS HEIR, HAD THIS PUT UP.
(Brixia is now Brescia in Northern Italy.)

THE LATER SECOND AND EARLY THIRD CENTURIES

THE NEW DEFENCES

In this period the early second-century curtain wall appears to have been replaced with a new wall, impressive lengths of which survive to this day, incorporated within the medieval City Wall on the north and east sides. Like the structure it replaced, this new wall was designed as a facing to the rampart behind, but it was of superlative construction. It consisted of thirteen courses of carefully matched and very large blocks of locally quarried sandstone set on a chamfered plinth. A fine decorative cornice and crenellated parapet were set on top, and the whole structure was approximately twenty-two feet (6.70 metres) high. The earlier towers were extensively remodelled and incorporated within the new defences. The defensive ditch was recut. It now seems possible that as part of this work the gates were rebuilt to a new, more impressive design, with semi-circular towers projecting beyond the front of the curtain wall.

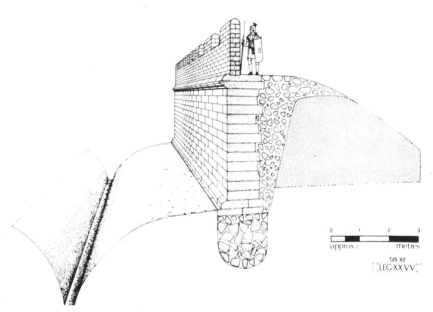

Above: The structure of the new defences *c.* AD 200.

Left: From AD 213-222 the Twentieth Legion was styled 'ANTONINIANA'. Tiles were stamped 'ANTO' accordingly.

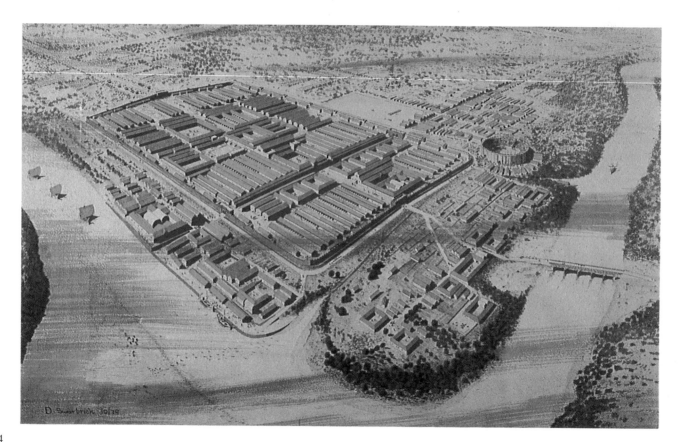

D. Swarbrick. 30/78

Above: The eagle-bearer of *Legio XX Valeria Victrix*. (C. Constable)

Opposite: How the fortress and town of *Deva* might have appeared in the early third century. (D. Swarbrick)

Left: Sarmatian cavalry. These men came from beyond the Danube and were drafted to Britain in the later second century. (G. Sumner)

Tombstone of a Sarmatian trooper.

Right, below: This wall of a senior centurion's house was completed *c.* AD 200. Note the earlier unfinished masonry below.

THE FORTRESS IN FULL USE

During the next sixty years or so the fortress at Chester was occupied intensively. Every part of it was affected. The cook-houses experienced their phase of most intensive use, the barracks were systematically rebuilt, or completed, as half-timber buldings on stone wall-sills, the granaries were rebuilt and at least one new granary was provided. New drains were laid down, and the major buildings (headquarters, legionary commander's palace, baths, hospital, etc.) were extensively rebuilt or repaired, with various minor internal alterations or improvements carried out. The strange Elliptical Building, whose exact function still remains unknown, was completed, and to its north a brand new stores depot was constructed.

All this activity attests a renewed impetus lasting into the early third century, and it is therefore not surprising that many of the Roman inscriptions which survive in Chester today were put up in this period. If ever there was a hey-day of Roman Chester, this was surely the time.

A cook-house stove *c.* AD 200.

LEGIONARY DETACHMENTS ON DUTY ELSEWHERE

Despite all this activity, it would be a mistake to imagine the entire Twentieth Legion present in Chester except on rare occasions. The legionary fortress served as a depot and administrative headquarters, and it would be quite normal for large detachments of legionaries *(Vexillationes)* — frequently thousands of men strong — to be absent on more or less permanent duties elsewhere, and not only in Britain. Incidentally, this may be the real explanation of the presence in Chester of at least one man from *Legio II Augusta* (Second Augustan Legion), whose depot was at Caerleon *(Isca)* in South Wales. It may be that he, and others like him, were on detached duties when he died in the early third century.

THE DEFENCES EXPLAINED

As depots, the fortresses were 'defended' in the way that our own regimental depots have been 'defended' in modern times, particularly in the later nineteenth century, with high walls, impressive gates and sentry boxes. Such walls have more to do with sound military practices and discipline than with actual defence against an enemy. On all but the rarest occasions during the first two centuries of the Roman fortress, no such enemies existed anywhere within hundreds of miles. No doubt, however, the defences did serve as an 'insurance policy'.

During this period the Chester Command covered north Wales, the whole of Cheshire, Lancashire as far as the Ribble, and much of Derbyshire.

Culvert of a main road in the fortress.

Left: A centurion's lead-lined private latrine.

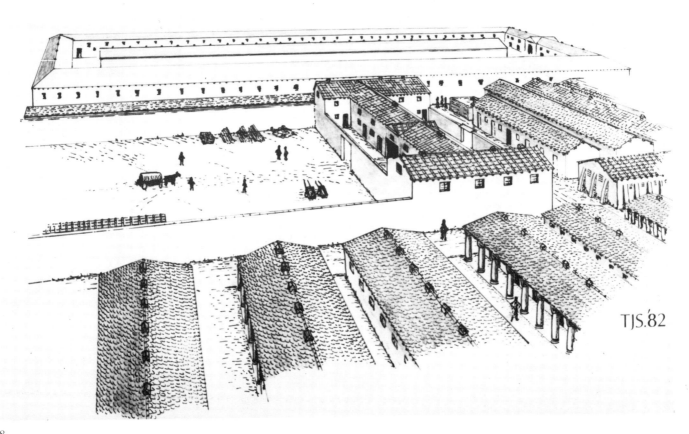

TJS.82

CHAPTER FOUR: THE FORTRESS IN THE LATER THIRD AND FOURTH CENTURIES

THE LAST EVIDENCE OF THE TWENTIETH LEGION

Inscriptions and stamped tiles made at Holt and used at Chester confirm that *Deva* was still the depot of the Twentieth Legion *c.* AD 250. However, during the third century, as in earlier periods, large detachments of men from the Twentieth are known to have been elsewhere, frequently brigaded with detachments from other legions. Thus, for example, in AD 255 part of the Twentieth is known to have been at Mainz, on the Rhine frontier, together with men from the Second Augustan Legion. A few years later, men of the Twentieth were on the Danube frontier. An inscribed altar was erected in one of the milecastles on Hadrian's Wall by men of the legion in AD 262-6. Towards the end of the third century the Twentieth Legion is named on some of the coins of the usurper Carausius, but this need not imply anything more than that part of the legion was under his control, and not necessarily at Chester or even in Britain. Coins of Carausius and other emperors of the later third century are, however, present in sufficient numbers in Chester to imply that the fortress remained a place of some significance, although not necessarily any longer as the base of the Twentieth Legion. Indeed, there is no positive proof of the presence of the legion at Chester after *c.* AD 250.

Right: Coin of Carausius, AD 287-295.

Below: During the reign of the Emperor Trajan Decius the Twentieth Legion was styled 'DECIANA'. Tiles stamped accordingly 'DE' give the latest proof of the legion at Chester.

Opposite: The heart of the fortress in the early third century: barracks (foreground), stores building (centre), and what may have been the hospital (background).

29

Third-century barrack roofing (restored).

Collapsed roofing on the site of a barrack *c.* AD 300.

THE END OF LEGIONARY OCCUPATION?

Many of the barracks had been in use down to about the middle of the century, at which time certain buildings, for example some of the fortress granaries, were being repaired, but between *c.* AD 250 and *c.* AD 300 (it is not yet possible to be more precise) barracks in widespread parts of the fortress appear to have become redundant. Ultimately, many of them appear to have been unoccupied whilst others were allowed to become derelict, until, in some cases, the roofing collapsed. This, too, seems to have happened to some of the granaries. In the same period some of the main drains had lost their capstones and were choked up. All this suggests that if Chester remained a military base, most if not all of the soldiers were absent elsewhere on a long-term basis.

On the other hand, major buildings such as the headquarters, baths, stores depot and hospital appear to have continued to be used, together with certain minor buildings such as a granary in the north-western part of the fortress. It is clear, therefore, that the fortress continued to be occupied. Chester may indeed have been ideally placed to be a base for the

Roman fleet dealing with an ever worsening situation due to increasing numbers of seaborne raiders; but, again, the proof of this is lacking. All that can be said is that whereas in the early third century Chester was clearly an intensively occupied legionary fortress, a hundred years later it was not.

Third-century bread ovens.

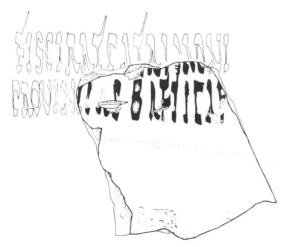

Fragment of amphora, for carrying olive oil from southern Spain. Translated, the label would have said:

> . . . pounds empty, merchandise of the financial department of the imperial estates of the province of Baetica, 216 pounds full.

Third century.

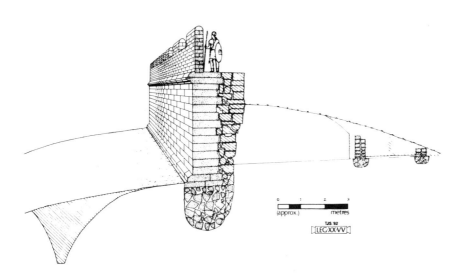

Reconstruction of the way in which the defences may
have been redesigned c. AD 300.
Note the reused stones behind the wall face.

THE FORTRESS IN THE FOURTH CENTURY

THE DEFENCES REDESIGNED

In AD 296 the Caesar Constantius Chlorus, together with his son Constantine, crossed the English Channel and thus brought to an end the independent empire of Carausius and his successor Allectus. In the years that followed, Constantius and his son campaigned in northern Britain and the country was subdivided into four small provinces. In this period the defences of Chester appear to have been systematically redesigned.

The curtain wall, which had been built by the Twentieth Legion in c. AD 200, was now made into a partially free-standing structure. To achieve this the rampart was reduced in height to form a wide low bank running over the sites of the now-dismantled cook-houses, and an inner face was added to the wall itself. The latter consisted largely of reused masonry. This was a widespread practice in this period, and a fortunate one, since it has led to the preservation and survival of a large number of earlier Roman tombstones and other carved and inscribed stones on which so much knowledge of the Roman period has depended.

Free-standing defensive walls were a common feature of late Roman military architecture, and Chester's wall is no exception. They are best explained by developments in military defensive tactics, for such walls had become 'defensive' in the fullest sense of the term.

The now reduced rampart could be mounted easily at any point on the circuit by a comparatively small garrison. The low earthen bank sloped gradually enough down to the gravel road within, even to allow for the possibility of moving heavy spring-guns and catapults up to the parapet-walk area.

THE FORTRESS INTERIOR

We have already seen that the major administrative and amenity buildings appear to have remained in use throughout this period. However, close study of the surviving buildings shows that their interiors had been much altered early in the fourth century. These alterations strongly indicate a change in the character of occupation of these buildings, if not a break with traditional functions.

Until recently it was thought that the legionary barracks had actually been systematically dismantled c.AD 300, but it is now realised that they continued to be used,

The gravel road inside the defences. Fourth century.

Coin of the Emperor Constantine. AD 308-337.

albeit in much altered form, after the late third-century 'break'. Coins and pottery show that more or less intensive occupation of the fortress continued thereafter down to the later years of the fourth century.

The floors of this large building close to the centre of the fortress were relaid with building debris after *c.* AD 300.

Gold coin of the Emperor Magnentius (AD 353), found in what had earlier been a possible legionary stores depot and which had been greatly altered in the fourth century.

THE STATUS OF CHESTER IN THE FOURTH CENTURY

What then of the status of Chester at this time? As said above, it was clearly important, and within the changed fabric of the Roman Army of the period it may, too, have retained a considerable military, though non-legionary, significance. In addition, changes in provincial organisation of Britain may have granted Chester a much enhanced political status. It has been suggested recently that from *c.* AD 340 it

had been raised to the position of capital of one of the five provinces into which Britain had by then been subdivided and, in addition, had become the headquarters of the *dux Britanniarum,* the army commander of the provinces of northern Britain. Soldiers at Chester appear to have been in receipt of pay from the imperial mints until the later 370s but no later Roman coinage has ever been found there. There are no coins of Magnus Maximus, despite his well-known historical and legendary connections with Britain.

Coin of the Emperor Valens, AD 364-378.

THE PEOPLE AND FUNCTIONS OF THE SETTLEMENT DESCRIBED

From the beginning of the permanent occupation of the site of Chester by the Roman Army, a settlement developed outside the walls of the fortress and mainly on the west, south and east sides. We can readily imagine the market forces which encouraged this development. In the early years there would, undoubtedly, have been a strong 'native' element consisting of those British tribesmen and their dependants who were able to make a living from providing the Roman soldiers with commodities and services of various kinds. There would, too, have been traders attracted to the place from all over the known world by the presence of soldiers with money to spend. It is not difficult to imagine the 'inns' and other places of entertainment which the soldiers would have frequented in their leisure hours. We should not forget that, in the first and second centuries, serving soldiers were not allowed to marry (this may seem strange to us today but not so long ago marriage was actively discouraged in the British Army) but there would, inevitably, have been attachments to local girls. When these men retired their 'marriages' were legalised.

There would, of course, have been a number of retired soldiers, many of whom would have had wives and children. Some of the men would have cornered small parts of the market in all sorts of commodities and amenities which they provided for their ex-companions. In the early days in particular, some of these people in the extramural settlement would have followed the legions to Chester from Lincoln and Wroxeter. There would also have been a certain official presence in the settlement; the coaching stations of the imperial post, the amphitheatre staff, customs officers and such like who would invariably have been retired soldiers or soldiers on 'secondment'. The men involved with the harbour facilities, warehouses, bath houses and the local quarries would have been additional elements. Permeating throughout this varied society would have been a number of slaves and servants. When they died, many of these people were buried in cemeteries outside the settlement, particularly alongside the main roads.

The Army of this period referred to such settlements as the 'canabae' which, loosely translated, means 'the hutments'. This was already a somewhat antiquated expression which colloquially had come to refer to that part of the extramural settlement which was under direct military supervision. This was frequently the responsibility of a senior legionary officer, the *praefectus castrorum* (camp prefect).

Less than two miles to the south of the fortress was a small but distinctly separate settlement at Heronbridge and this, in all likelihood, would not have been under military jurisdiction. Such outlying settlements were a well-known feature in the neighbourhood of the legionary fortresses throughout the Roman world.

THE LEGIONARY *PRATA*

In addition, the legion had what was known as the '*prata*' or 'pasture' and which, in some cases, formed part of what came later to be known as the '*territorium*' — a term which does not need translation. The *prata* would have been a large area of the surrounding countryside set aside for the provision, under direct military supervision, of pasture and fodder for the very large number of mounts, baggage and draught animals kept by the legion, and also, no doubt, for the provision of 'meat' on a large scale. It is clear from the archaeological excavations in Chester that the soldiers ate a very large quantity of meat of all descriptions, largely from domesticated animals such as cow, pig, sheep and goat, which attests a large-scale and highly organised farming system. The Army also provided the soldiers with a staple diet of grain of various kinds but this would have been imported from outside the area, frequently by sea. The soldiers supplemented their provisions through hunting and fishing.

THE RURAL COMMUNITY

In addition to the *prata* there would have been an independent rural community, sometimes concentrated in small farming villages, largely descended from the local tribesmen, to some extent making a living from the markets now provided by the soldiers and people of the *canabae* at Chester. Such settlements are known to have existed at Saltney, a mile or so to the south of the fortress, and another has been found very recently about ten miles further south, beside the main road to Whitchurch *(Mediolanum)*. There must also have been farmsteads and — as we now know from recent discoveries — a series of what have come to be known as 'villas', a few of which may have been the Roman equivalent of our houses

in the country. Many of the others would have been the centres of well-to-do farming estates and other farmsteads. In time the fortress acted as a centre of a local road system which developed to the point at which it cannot have been so very different from that which exists today.

A 'villa' in the countryside.

37

A tombstone of Greek freedmen or traders. Translated, it reads:

TO THE SPIRITS OF THE DEPARTED AND OF FLAVIUS CALLIMORPHUS, WHO LIVED 42 YEARS, AND OF SERAPION, WHO LIVED 3 YEARS, 6 MONTHS. THESAEUS HAD THIS PUT UP TO BROTHER AND SON.

THE *CANABAE* IN THE THIRD CENTURY

In the early third century, the Emperor Septimius Severus made it possible for serving soldiers to be legally married. Undoubtedly, this was done to make a military life more attractive to potential recruits, and thus make it easier to bring the army up to strength. It was also a tacit recognition of the soldiers' widespread practice of forming technically illegal attachments! At the same time — and this was probably not foreseen — it gave a boost to the *canabae*. Not long afterwards, Severus' son Caracalla extended citizenship to all free-born people in the Empire. It is perhaps for these reasons more than any others that the town outside the legionary fortress grew to its maximum extent in this period. At this time it covered almost the same area as did the City of Chester in the eighteenth century and, in addition to the legion itself, may have had a population of several thousand people.

THE LATE ROMAN TOWN

Inevitably, the fortunes of the *canabae* closely reflect those of the fortress to which it was so closely linked. However, with the widespread and fundamental changes which

took place inside the fortress during the third and early fourth centuries it is likely that the distinctions between fortress and extramural settlement became increasingly blurred. It is possible that the *canabae* achieved a considerable degree of independence from the Army which led, ultimately, to a complete reversal of the situation pertaining in the first and second centuries. In the end the garrison was part of a largely autonomous civilian establishment.

A well in an official posting house *(Mansio)* in the *Canabae*.

The quayside wall of the Roman waterfront.

CHAPTER SIX: CONTINUITY THROUGH THE DARK AGES

During the later fourth and early fifth centuries Britain was further subdivided into Kingdoms founded on late Roman political arrangements. Although direct government from Italy ceased during the early fifth century, Chester remained in that part of the country which fell under 'British', as distinct from 'Saxon', control for some time to come.

It is possible that Arthur — that is the Arthur of historical fact rather than the King of medieval romance — fought the ninth of his battles at or near Chester late in the fifth century, but it must be said that there is at least one other contender (Caerleon in South Wales) for the site of this battle. Certainly, however, there is no reason to doubt that Chester was still a place of some importance a hundred years later, a fact attested by the 'synod urb. legion' — the 'Synod of the city of the legion' in AD 603, at which the Bishops and learned men of the British Church met Saint Augustine. This is the subject of one of the most interesting and unambiguous Dark Age references to Chester in the Welsh Annals.

The last Dark Age — or rather 'sub-Roman' — reference to Chester is also dated to the early seventh century, some say AD 613, when Aethelfrith of Northumbria 'assembled a great army at the city of the legion' prior to a battle nearby in which, amongst other things, he is said to have slaughtered many of the monks from Bangor-on-Dee. It is not possible to assess the strategic significance, or otherwise, of this action. Nevertheless, these events point not only to Chester's continued political, ecclesiastical and strategic importance, but also to a degree of continuity in the urban population.

In this late period, with the fundamental breakdown in communications and the almost complete collapse of the international economy, large-scale manufacturing industry had ceased in Britain, and Roman coinage was no longer in circulation in the 'market-place'. So the archaeologist is almost completely denied the best dating evidence. However, at least two sites in Chester have recently produced a few sherds of very late Roman pottery imported from the eastern Mediterranean area which, on the one hand, demonstrates some form of continuity in the occupation of Chester and, on the other hand, that some at least of the local inhabitants were preserving trade links — probably by sea — with what remained of the Roman world. In addition to this important evidence there are fragmentary traces of buildings in different

Opposite: A simplified cross-section through the layers on a site in Chester showing the survival of a Roman building into the early Middle Ages.

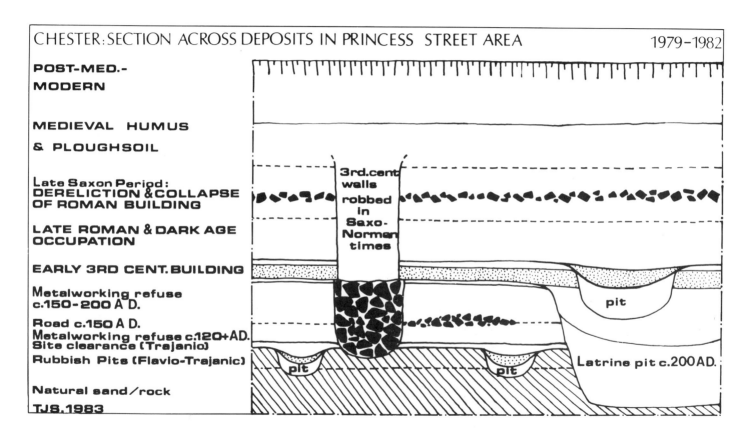

CHESTER: SECTION ACROSS DEPOSITS IN PRINCESS STREET AREA   1979-1982

POST-MED.-
MODERN

MEDIEVAL HUMUS
& PLOUGHSOIL

Late Saxon Period:
DERELICTION & COLLAPSE
OF ROMAN BUILDING

LATE ROMAN & DARK AGE
OCCUPATION

EARLY 3RD CENT. BUILDING

Metalworking refuse
c.150-200 A.D.

Road c.150 A.D.
Metalworking refuse c.120+ A.D.
Site clearance (Trajanic)
Rubbish Pits (Flavio-Trajanic)

Natural sand/rock

TJS.1983

3rd. cent. walls robbed in Saxo-Norman times

pit

pit   pit

Latrine pit c.200 A.D.

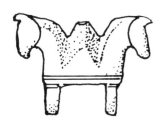

A lead trial-piece for a Dark Age horse-headed buckle ornament, found on the site of a legionary barrack block. Such objects were usually worn by women. Of British manufacture, their design exhibits Germanic influences. (max. width 27mm.)

parts of Chester which almost certainly belong to this period, but which cannot be closely dated or fully interpreted until much more is known. We do know, however, that by the middle of the eighth century Chester belonged within the emerging Saxon Kingdom of Mercia, and society had by then developed into that mixture of racial strains, and cultural styles, which has come to be known as 'English'. In one sense, therefore, Roman Chester had come to an end. It had evolved into something different, or at least no longer recognisably 'Roman'.

A tenth-century Viking brooch found in the remains of a Roman building. (Diam. 32mm.)

In another very real way, however, Roman Chester survived for hundreds of years to come. In 1981, large-scale excavations in the city centre confirmed something which had long been suspected hitherto, but for which the proof had been lacking; that much of the fabric of the Roman fortress and town remained upstanding and largely intact, although in increasingly ruinous condition, until the Middle Ages. So much so that it has influenced the plan of Chester ever since, just as it will continue to do into the future. On this final note it is fitting that we should recall what Ranulf Higden, a monk of the Abbey of Saint Werburgh, was able to say in the fourteenth century, as he gazed in awe at the physical remains of a great civilization:

When I behold the ground-work of buildings in the streets, laid with main strong huge stones, it seemeth that it hath been founded by the painful labour of Romans, or giants . . .

EN FRANÇAIS

Les Romains connurent le site de Chester et ils s'en servirent à plusieurs occasions, à un certain temps avant la construction de la forteresse de la légion vers la fin des ans AD 70. Une rivière navigable, de bonnes communications par terre et un emplacement stratégique donnèrent tous au site une influence considérable. La première forteresse, construite de *LEGIO II ADIUTRIX* (la Deuxième Légion 'Auxiliaire') était d'une construction en grande mesure de bois. Cette légion fut remplacée par *LEGIO XX VALERIA VICTRIX* (La Vingtième Légion Courageuse et Victorieuse) tout à la fin du premier siècle. Au début du 2e siècle, la reconstruction de la forteresse prit fin lorsque la 20e légion fut détachée pour aider à construire le Mur d'Hadrien et plus tard le Mur d'Antoninus. Vers la fin 2e siècle et au commencement du 3e siècle, la forteresse fut terminée et elle fut intensivement occupée. La dernière preuve de l'occupation de Chester par la légion est datée *c.*AD 250 et c'est bien probable que la légion n'y était plus en résidence au début de l'an AD 300. Néanmoins, Chester jouait un rôle encore important et on y apporta des améliorations aux défenses.

Pendant l'époque romaine et en particulier vers la fin du 2e siècle et au début du 3e siècle, une grande colonie se développa à l'extérieur des murs d'enceinte de la forteresse du côté ouest, sud et est. Sa population crût en nombre à plusieurs milliers de gens. Il y avait des colonies périphériques et une grande communauté rurale. Au 4e siécle les distinctions entre la forteresse et la ville s'estompèrent. Il se peut qu'à cette époque Chester fût devenue la capitale de province et le quartier général du commandant militaire de la Bretagne du Nord.

Bien que le gouvernement romain se fût arrêté au début du 5e siécle, le Chester 'romain' continua pendant quelque temps. La ville ne tomba aux mains des Saxons qu'au 8e siècle. Beaucoup de la structure romaine de Chester survécut au suprême degré au Moyen Âge. Depuis ce moment–là Le plan de la cité de Chester en a été influencé.

AUF DEUTSCH

Die Lage von Chester war den Römern bekannt und sie wurde von ihnen bemehreren Gelegenheiten benutzt, irgendwann, bevor die Festung der Legion in den späten Jahren AD 70 gebaut worden war. Wegen eines schiffbaren Flusses, guter Kommunikationen auf dem Landweg und eines strategischen Standortes ist die Lage wichtig geworden. Die erste Festung ist von der *LEGIO II ADIUTRIX* (der Zweiten Hilfslegion) zum grössten Teil aus Holz erbaut worden. Diese Legion ist am Ende des ersten Jahrhunderts von der *LEGIO XX VALERIA VICTRIX* (der Mutigen und Siegreichen Zwanzigsten Legion) ersetzt worden. Im frühen 2. jahrhundert ist der Wiederaufbau der Festung zu Ende gebracht worden, als die Zwanzigste Legion abkommandiert wurde, um beim Bau vom Hadrianswall und später vom Antoninswall zu helfen. Gegen Ende des 2. Jahrhunderts und auch im frühen 3. Jahrhundert ist die Festung fertiggestellt und intensiv besetzt worden. Der neueste Beweis der Legionokkupation in Chester datiert *c.* AD 250 zurück und vor dem Anfang des Jahres AD 300 war die Legion wahrscheinlich nicht mehr anwesend. Chester war, aber, noch wichtig und man führte verschiedene Verbesserungen an den Befestigungen durch.

Während der römischen Epoche und besonders während des späten 2. Jahrhunderts und des frühen 3. Jahrhunderts hat sich eine grosse Siedlung ausserhalb der Festungmauer auf der Westen =, Süden = und Ostenseite entwickelt. Es waren mehrere tausend Leute in dieser Siedlung. Es waren auch Aussensiedlungen und auch eine grosse Landgemeinde. Im 4. Jahrhundert wurden die Unterscheidungen zwischen der Festung und der Stadt undeutlich. Zu dieser Zeit könnte es sein, dass Chester die Provinzhauptstadt und das Hauptquartier für den Militärkommandant von Nordbritannien.

Obgleich die römische Regierung im frühen 5. Jahrhundert geendet hat, hat die römische Stadt von Chester nachher angedauert. Sie ist erst das 8. Jahrhundert in die Hände der Sachsen gefallen. Viel von der Struktur der römischen Chester dauerte in hohem Masse ins Mittelalter über. Sie hat seither den Stadtplan von Chester beeinflusst.

CHRONOLOGICAL TABLE OF ROMAN BRITAIN
Events of significance at Chester in bold type

AD 43-7	Romans invade Britain and advance to the Midlands.
47-59	Campaigns in Wales. **Forts/fortresses at *Deva*?**
60	Rebellion of British tribes under Boudicca.
71-4	Conquest of Brigantia. **Arrival of Legion II Adiutrix.**
74	**Deceanglian (North Wales) lead mines in operation.**
74-9	Final conquest of Wales. **Legionary fortress under construction (partly in stone) at *Deva*.**
80-*c*. 90	Shift of warfare to the North.
c. 90-100	Withdrawal from Scotland. **Legion XX replaces Legion II Adiutrix at *Deva*. Renewed impetus to stone building programme.**
122	Hadrian visits Britain. Construction of Hadrian's Wall begins. **Detachments from Legion XX on duty in the North.**
c. 140	Construction of Antonine Wall (Forth-Clyde).
c. 160	Withdrawal from Scotland. **Fortress at *Deva* reoccupied in strength. Further building and alterations.**
c. 200-211	Severus reorganises Britain. **Rebuilding programme commences at *Deva*. Elliptical building completed. Defences rebuilt.**
259-274	The Gallic Empire. **Last proof of Legion XX in Britain.**

283-296	Britain under Carausius and Allectus. **Legion XX no longer at *Deva?***
296-	Constantius restores 'the Eternal Light'.
c. 300	Britain reorganised. **Widespread dereliction of legionary buildings at *Deva?***
306	Constantine proclaimed Emperor at York.
c. 340	Constans reorganises the coastal defences. ***Deva* re-garrisoned? Many timber buildings erected at *Deva*. HQ of Dux Britanniarum?**
c. 350	Magnentius. **Some troops withdrawn from *Deva?***
367	The Great Barbarian Conspiracy.
370s	**End of miliary occupation of *Deva?***
c. 400	Stilicho repulses Picts, Scots and Saxons.
410	End of direct Roman rule in Britain.
c. 430	Cunedda recovers N. Wales from the Scots, **perhaps using *Deva* as a base.**
449	Hengest and Horsa invited in as mercenaries.
c. 450-*c.* 500	Arthur. **Ninth battle at City of Legions (*Deva?*)**
603	**Synod of the City of Legions. St. Augustine meets the Celtic bishops at Chester.**
613	**Aethelfrith of Northumbria assembles a great army at the City of Legions. British forces defeated near Chester.**

SELECT BOOKLIST

ROMAN BRITAIN IN GENERAL

ALCOCK, L., *Arthur's Britain*. Penguin Books, 1971. A good guide to modern scholarly interpretation of the sources of information for Dark Age Britain.

FRERE, S.S., *Britannia: A History of Roman Britain*. Second, revised edition, Sphere Books, 1974.

SALWAY, P., *Roman Britain*. Oxford University Press, 1981. The latest standard text book.

WEBSTER, G., *The Roman Imperial Army*. A. & C. Black Ltd., 1969, with subsequent revised editions. The standard account of the Roman Army of the late first and early second centuries AD.

WEBSTER, G., *Boudicca*. Batsford Ltd., 1978. A fascinating up-to-date account of the rebellion of AD 60, its causes and aftermath.

WEBSTER, G., *Rome against Caratacus*. Book Club Associates, 1981. The latest thinking on Roman campaigns in Britain in the middle of the first century AD.

ROMAN CHESHIRE AND THE REGION

BU'LOCK, J. D., *Pre-Conquest Cheshire 383-1066*. Cheshire Community Council, 1972. A gathering together of much of the evidence for Cheshire in the Dark Ages.

THOMPSON, F. H., *Roman Cheshire*. Cheshire Community Council, 1965. Still perhaps the best guide although now somewhat out of date. Now out of print.

WATKIN, W. T., *Roman Cheshire*. Produced originally in 1888, a reprinted edition with new introduction by D. F. Petch was published by E. P. Publishing, Ltd., Wakefield, in 1974. Although out of date in certain matters of interpretation, this is still a fascinating and invaluable collection of information, indispensible to the serious student.

WEBSTER, G., *The Cornovii*. Duckworth, 1975. A good general historical account of the region to the south of Chester, with some emphasis on early military campaigns in the region, the Cornovian tribal capital at Wroxeter, and a fascinating résumé of latest evidence for the disintegration of Roman Britain in the Dark Ages.

NASH - WILLIAMS, V. E., *The Roman Frontier in Wales*. Revision edited by M. G. Jarrett, University of Wales Press (Cardiff), 1969. Now out of print but essential reading for the serious student.

COLLINGWOOD, R. G. and WRIGHT, R. P., 'The Roman Inscriptions in the Grosvenor Museum, Chester', from *The Roman Inscriptions of Britain, I,* Oxford University Press, 1965. Reprinted, with addenda by G. Lloyd-Morgan and D. J. Robinson of the Grosvenor Museum, Chester, 1978. The definitive account, with translations and interpretation.

MASON, D. J. P., *Chester Excavations: 11-15 Castle Street and Neighbouring Sites 1974-8: A Possible Roman Posting House.* Grosvenor Museum, Chester 1980.

PETCH, D. F., *Deva Victrix.* Ginn & Co. Ltd., 1971. Although out of date in some respects, this is still the best general guide to Roman Chester and its surviving visible remains. Out of print.

STRICKLAND, T. J. and DAVEY, P. J. (eds.) *New Evidence for Roman Chester.* Liverpool University, 1978. Includes much of the latest evidence and interpretation.

STRICKLAND, T. J., 'Third Century Chester'. A contribution to *The Roman West In The Third Century* edited by A. King and M. Henig. British Archaeological Reports, 1981. The most up-to-date gathering-together of the archaeological evidence.

THOMPSON, F. H., 'Excavation of the Roman Amphitheatre at Chester'. Volume CV, *Archaeologia,* the Journal of the Society of Antiquaries of London, 1976.

WARD, S. and STRICKLAND, T. J., *Chester Excavations: Northgate Brewery 1974-5; A Roman Centurion's Quarter and Barrack.* Grosvenor Museum, Chester 1978.

In addition to these, there are a number of important articles in the *Journal of the Chester Archaeological Society.* See also the *Annals of Archaeology and Anthropology of the University of Liverpool,* the *Cheshire Archaeological Bulletin, Britannia* (the Journal of the Society for the Promotion of Roman Studies), monographs and newsletters published by the Grosvenor Museum, Chester. Volume I of the *Victoria History of Cheshire,* publication of which is expected in 1985, will contain an article on Roman Cheshire by D. F. Petch.